D0948164

FAMOUS LIVES

The Story of
JUNÍPERO SERRA
Brave Adventurer

FAMOUS LIVES

titles in Large-Print Editions:

FAMOUS LIVES

The Story of
JUNÍPERO SERRA
Brave Adventurer

By Florence Meiman White
Illustrated By Stephen Marchesi

Gareth Stevens Publishing
MILWAUKEE

PUBLIC LIBRARY
EAST ORANGE, NEW JERSEY

jB   8/96
cop. 1

For a free color catalog describing Gareth Stevens' list of high-quality books, call 1-800-542-2595 (USA) or 1-800-461-9120 (Canada). Gareth Stevens' Fax: (414) 225-0377.

Library of Congress Cataloging-in-Publication Data

White, Florence Meiman, 1910-.
    The story of Junípero Serra: brave adventurer / by Florence
Meiman White ; illustrated by Stephen Marchesi.
       p. cm. — (Famous lives)
    Includes index.
    Summary: Presents the life story of the intrepid Franciscan missionary
and explorer who established the first nine missions in California and
devoted his life to working with the Indians.
    ISBN 0-8368-1460-6
    1. Serra, Junípero, 1713-1784—Juvenile literature. 2. Explorers—
California—Biography—Juvenile literature. 3. Explorers—Spain—
Biography—Juvenile literature. 4. Franciscans—California—
Biography—Juvenile literature. 5. Franciscans—Missions—California—
History—18th century—Juvenile literature. 6. Indians of North
America—Missions—California—Juvenile literature. 7. California—
History—To 1846—Juvenile literature. [1. Serra, Junípero, 1713-1784.
2. Explorers. 3. Missionaries. 4. Indians of North America—
Missions—California. 5. California—History—To 1846.] I. Marchesi,
Stephen, ill. II. Title. III. Series: Famous lives (Milwaukee, Wis.).
F864.S44W48   1996
979.4'02.'092—dc20   95-36842
[B]

The events described in this book are true. They have been carefully researched and excerpted from authentic biographies, writings, and commentaries. No part of this biography has been fictionalized. To learn more about Father Junípero Serra and the history of California, refer to the list of books and videos at the back of this book or ask your librarian to recommend other fine books and videos.

This edition first published in 1996 by
Gareth Stevens Publishing
1555 North RiverCenter Drive, Suite 201
Milwaukee, Wisconsin 53212, USA

Original © 1987 by Parachute Press, Inc. as a Yearling Biography.
Published by arrangement with Bantam Doubleday Dell Books for Young Readers,
a division of Bantam Doubleday Dell Publishing Group, Inc.
Additional end matter © 1996 by Gareth Stevens, Inc.

The trademark Yearling® is registered in the U.S. Patent and Trademark Office.
The trademark Dell® is registered in the U.S. Patent and Trademark Office.

All rights to this edition reserved to Gareth Stevens, Inc. No part of this book may be reproduced, stored in a retrieval system, or transmitted in any form or by any means, electronic, mechanical, photocopying, recording, or otherwise without the prior written permission of the publisher except for the inclusion of brief quotations in an acknowledged review.

Printed in the United States of America

1 2 3 4 5 6 7 8 9 99 98 97 96

To the memory of my mother and father
and
To George Nicholson
whose interest in Father Serra
prompted the writing of this book

Contents

FAMOUS LIVES

The Story of
JUNÍPERO SERRA
Brave Adventurer

Introduction

AFTER COLUMBUS CAME TO THE NEW World, the exciting age of exploration and discovery began. During the 1500s Spain grew into a mighty empire. Courageous and daring Spaniards, eager to discover new trade routes and to conquer new lands for their king, ventured across the oceans in their Spanish galleons. Before the English came to Jamestown, Virginia, in 1607, Spain possessed most of South America, some of the southern part of North America, and many islands in the Caribbean Sea.

11

In 1542 navigator Juan Cabrillo visited the beautiful golden wilderness with its majestic, rugged mountains on America's West Coast—California—and he claimed San Diego for Spain. Then in 1602 an explorer named Sebastián Vizcaino, in search of a harbor for ships coming from as far away as the Philippines, found and claimed the beautiful and serene Monterey Bay. After that—for one hundred seventy-five years—California remained undisturbed.

Then in 1769 the Spanish leader José de Gálvez decided to send colonists to California so it could officially belong to Spain. Gálvez organized a great expedition comprising valiant soldiers and missionaries and told them to honor the claims of both Cabrillo and Vizcaino by colonizing the land from San Diego to Monterey Bay.

One very brave missionary and pioneer to California was Father Junípero Serra. He was responsible for helping to set up and maintain California's first missions. These were small communities where many Indians lived, worked, and prayed at the mission churches.

Father Serra's long trek to California was difficult and dangerous. But he had a motto: "Always go forward. Never turn back." This is the story of how Father Junípero Serra lived those words.

Spain

FASTER AND FASTER! THE TWO MEN PAD-dled their canoe over the dangerous river. Angry alligators bellowed in the waters below. But the two men could not stop to rest. Nearby, along the river banks of the thick jungle, lions and tigers roared. Poisonous snakes slithered across the ground.

These two brave adventurers were Franciscan priests. They were on their way to a village in Mexico to teach the Indians about the Christian religion. Nothing could stop them. They had to keep going—and they did—over scorching deserts and through high steep mountains until they completed their mission. One of these men was Father Junípero Serra.

After midnight on November 24, 1713, a baby boy was born to Antonio and Margarita Serra. The baby was so small and weak-looking that his father was afraid he would die before he became a Christian. So Antonio Serra decided not to wait to have his baby baptized. As soon as the sun came up, he rushed his son to church. There the infant was baptized and named Miguel José Serra.

As a child, Miguel Serra lived in a small stone cottage on a narrow street in the village of Petra. The street was so narrow that a modern car would have trouble getting through it. But it was just right for stretching a line from one side to the other to hang the family wash.

Antonio Serra was a poor, hard-working farmer. Donkeys were kept in Antonio's stable a few steps from the house. While Margarita and her daughter worked in the house, Miguel carried water from the village pump. He took the animals to pasture and helped his father with the farm work.

Early in the morning Antonio and the other farmers would walk to their small fields a distance from their homes. Their young sons bumped along in a cart drawn by a gentle donkey. While the fathers plowed and planted, the boys brought food and water, gathered firewood, and did other small chores. Although Miguel was smaller than most boys his age, and not very strong, he tried to do as much as the others.

The Serra family was very religious. Every evening of her life, Margarita went to church. From the time Miguel was able to walk, she took him along with her. He quickly learned the prayers, and he loved singing hymns.

Most children did not go to school at that time, but Miguel was lucky. Because he was smart and because he was not strong enough to work on the farm, his parents wanted him to get an education. So they sent him to a religious school in Petra. Miguel's teachers

were Franciscan priests, and they taught him religion, history, geography, and Latin. Miguel loved to read and was the best reader in his class.

When Miguel finished school in Petra, he decided to become a priest. He needed more education to become a priest, so his teachers advised him to go to Lullian University in the city of Palma.

Miguel's parents were troubled. They could not afford to send their son to a university. But their fears were quickly put to rest. The Lullian University did not require tuition from poor people. Since Miguel was intelligent and a good student, he was quickly accepted into the school.

The day Miguel left for the university, he kissed his mother and sister good-bye and put a small pack of clothes on his back. Then he and his father, Antonio, walked the twenty-five miles to Palma. This would be the first of many long journeys for Miguel. When they got there, Antonio arranged for his son to live at the home of a priest.

After he entered, Miguel Serra soon began

to have trouble at the university. He was small for his age, and he looked very young. His teachers didn't believe he was old enough to be a university student or to prepare to be a Franciscan friar. Some students accused him of lying about his age and would have nothing to do with him.

But soon Miguel Serra proved to be one of the university's best students. When he was only sixteen years old, he was given permission to prepare for the priesthood. He helped out in the church by serving daily mass. But he wasn't allowed to sing in the choir because he was too short to reach the choir rack.

Miguel's favorite books were about the lives of the saints. He especially liked Saint Francis who had started the order of Franciscan Friars. St. Francis was rich, but gave away his wealth and lived with the poor. He believed that all men were brothers and should help one another. Miguel Serra was also inspired by saints who had gone to far-away places to teach the Christian religion to non-Christians.

When Miguel was seventeen, he became a priest and a member of the order of Franciscan Friars. On the day he took his vows as a priest, he changed his name to Junípero, after a jolly friar who had been a follower of Saint Francis. Junípero had been so devoted to the poor that he often gave away all of his food. One day he even gave away his robe to a beggar and was left standing stark naked!

After the young Father Junípero Serra became a priest, he was assigned to teach philosophy at the university and to work in neighborhood churches. But his real dream was to cross the Atlantic Ocean and convert the Indians in the New World. The church was sending missionaries there, and Father Serra was eager to go.

But the head of the church refused to send him. He thought Father Serra was too valuable a teacher to lose. Father Serra was very disappointed, but he decided it must be God's will that he wait before becoming a missionary in the New World.

He remained in Palma, teaching philosophy and gaining fame as an outstanding preacher. He had a deep, wonderful voice, and he spoke with great ease. Though he was a small man, only five feet two inches tall, everyone admired and respected him.

Then in 1749 a group of Franciscan Friars was preparing to sail for Mexico. Some of the friars had heard that crossing the Atlantic could be very dangerous. They were too afraid to make the trip and refused to go.

When Father Junípero Serra heard that others were needed to take the places of the fearful friars, he quickly volunteered. He also talked his best friend and former student, Father Francisco Palou, into going with him.

This time the head of the church did not interfere. At the age of thirty-six, after waiting twenty years, Father Serra was about to see his dream of becoming a missionary in the New World come true.

Journey to the New World

IN AUGUST OF 1749 FATHER SERRA AND FAther Palou set sail across the Atlantic with nineteen other friars. Strong winds and torrential storms tossed the small crowded ship as if it were a toy boat in a bathtub. Some days the harsh winds drove the ship off course. Other days, when the wind died, the ship's sails hung limply in the still air.

The passengers and crew suffered from seasickness and from a shortage of food and water. Father Serra was the only one who did not get sick. He tried to limit the amount of water he drank. When asked if he was thirsty, he answered, "It is nothing to worry about. I have found a way to avoid thirst, and it is this: to eat little and talk less and so save my saliva."

After more than three months at sea, the ship finally arrived at the port of Vera Cruz in Mexico. Father Serra and the others were welcomed by priests there, who gave them food and shelter.

While in Vera Cruz Father Palou became ill with a high fever. After a few days Serra had to bid farewell to his good friend, who was still too sick to travel. Serra and the other priests were ready to begin another long journey—three hundred miles—to the College of San Fernando in Mexico City, where they would study and prepare for their missionary work.

Most of the friars traveled on mules to Mexico City, but Junípero Serra refused to ride. He said that he would walk as Saint Francis would have. Wearing his gray woolen robe, with leather sandals on his feet and an old prayer book in his hands, he set out on foot with another friar, Father Pedro. The two priests carried neither food nor water. Father Serra believed that since God watched over them, kind people would help them along the way.

The road from Vera Cruz to Mexico City was nearly as dangerous as the Atlantic Ocean had been. The friars crossed deep rivers and climbed steep mountains. They passed through jungle, desert, and forest. Some days it was so hot, they could barely walk. In spite of all the hardships, they traveled about twenty miles a day.

Sometimes Father Serra and Father Pedro found wild berries along the trails and cold water from springs. But some days they found nothing. One day a stranger on horseback gave them each a loaf of delicious bread. Another time a man gave them some pomegranates. These fruits with their red, tart berries served as both food and drink for the friars and gave them the energy to go on.

Then one night in a tropical jungle, a

small creature bit Father Serra on the leg and caused him great pain. To this day no one knows for sure whether it was a poisonous mosquito, chigger, or spider. Whatever the creature was, it caused him great suffering throughout the rest of his life.

The next morning he was still in pain. The men were miles away from a town or a doctor. So, leaning on the arm of Father Pedro, Serra limped along the road until they came to a small cabin, where he could rest.

The following day the bite was a big open sore, and Father Serra's leg was swollen to almost twice its size. Father Pedro washed his friend's leg and begged him to rest. But Serra could only be talked into resting for one night. He did not want to delay the rest of their journey.

The next day the determined priest was back on the road, dragging his leg over sand and rock. The two friars still had at least fifty miles to travel.

Two days later, on January 1, 1750, Fa-

ther Serra limped through the gates of the College of San Fernando in Mexico City with Father Pedro. Both men were exhausted, and Serra's leg throbbed with pain, but they *had* arrived!

Mexico

EVERYONE AT THE COLLEGE HAD HEARD about the little priest from Spain. They knew that he was a brilliant scholar, and they wanted to treat him like someone very special. But Father Serra wouldn't hear of it. He insisted on being treated like everyone else. Although his leg still bothered him, he was eager to get on with his studies.

Friars usually spent a year studying and training for missionary work before they were sent out in the field. The college tried to prepare them for the hardships and loneliness of frontier life. But Father Serra had been in training only five months when the director of the college announced that missionaries were needed to work with the Pame Indians in Sierra Gorda.

The director had previously sent priests to set up missions in Sierra Gorda. Now both priests and Indians were starving. Their crops had failed, and although the priests often went hungry trying to make sure the Indians were fed, there just wasn't enough food. Then an epidemic broke out. A few priests died. Those who were ill had to return to the college. Two thirds of the Indians also died.

Many Indians ran away from the missions and returned to their life in the woods. They thought their gods had brought on the illness to punish them for abandoning their ancient beliefs. Some of the Pames ran away because they didn't trust the Spanish soldiers who protected the missions. Whenever a musket shot was fired, the Indians would become frightened.

After learning about the terrible conditions in Sierra Gorda and knowing that a dangerous trip lay ahead, Father Serra was still eager to go. He was eager to begin his missionary work. "Here I am. Send me!" he said to the director of the college.

Father Serra was given permission to go to one of the missions. So was his best friend, Father Palou, who had recovered from his illness in Vera Cruz and was now at the college.

Sierra Gorda was located high in a craggy mountain range over two hundred miles from Mexico City. The roads to Sierra Gorda were muddy and treacherous. Most were nearly impassable because of the torrential summer rains. The harsh heat and dampness made Father Serra's bad leg swell painfully as he and Palou trudged through slimy swamps and over rugged mountains.

When the two priests arrived at the mission, they immediately went to work to improve conditions. Father Serra understood that before he could convert the Indians, he had to make sure they had enough food to eat and clothes to wear.

The Indians had always gotten their food

by hunting and fishing, and by gathering fruits from the trees and seeds from the ground. Father Serra showed them other ways to get food. He asked that bulls and cows and sheep be sent to the mission. He showed the Indians how to care for the animals so that there would be meat for the children when the hunting was poor. Father Serra sent for maize and beans and showed the Indians how to plant. He also taught the women how to cook the crops they harvested, and he taught them how to weave and sew.

Father Serra began studying the Pame language so that he could pray with the Indians in their language. He even wrote a simple catechism in their language.

The priest grew very attached to the Pame children. He often gathered them together and taught them hymns and prayers. He told them stories about the lives of the saints. He helped them put on a play at Christmas. The Indian boys and girls dressed as angels and acted out the story of the birth of Jesus.

The children knelt about a real baby, lying in a manger.

Father Serra introduced other Catholic celebrations to the Pame Indians. Every Saturday night he organized a grand march. Holding a statue of the Holy Mother and the baby Jesus, he led the parade through the village. The children followed with their parents. They carried flaming torches to light the night, and they carried bright banners painted with pictures of the saints.

Many of the Indians, especially the women, liked this new way of life at the mission, and they told their friends about it. More and more Indians came to the mission and became Christians. Father Serra called these new Christians "neophytes."

With all the new converts, the old adobe church with a thatched roof was too small. Together Serra and the Indians began building a new stone church. In tattered clothing the priest often worked alongside the Indians, lifting heavy beams and filling the crevices between the stones. Working only in the dry season when they didn't have to do farmwork, it took seven years for the church to be completed. Four other stone missions were also built in surrounding areas The director of the College of San Fernando was greatly impressed by the fine work that Father Serra was doing in Sierra Gorda and appointed him Father President of the region. Now hard-working Serra had the responsibility of supervising all the missions in the area.

Junípero Serra lived and worked with the Pame Indians for eight and a half years. Then the college director sent word that he was needed back in Mexico City. The Pames didn't want him to leave, but the priest had to follow orders. Sadly, in 1758, he took leave of the people he'd grown to love and returned to the college in Mexico City.

In 1519 the Spanish explorer Hernando Cortez had conquered Mexico and named it New Spain. The conquerers found many treasures of gold in Mexico and took them back to Spain. After that many Spaniards migrated to Mexico.

Now, in the middle of the 1700s, Mexico City was filled with four groups of people. The high government officials were the recent arrivals from Spain. They were the rich and noble class. The Spaniards who were born in the New World made up the middle class. Blacks and mixed bloods or *mestizos* were still another group. They were poor, but the poorest of all were the Native Indians.

It was very difficult for Father Serra to accept the vast differences between the lives of the rich and the very poor. He did not enjoy preaching to the rich in Mexico City. The women often came to church dressed in diamonds and rubies. Sometimes during a service, the women would order their servants to bring them cups of chocolate. Father Serra considered this rude behavior which showed a lack of respect for the church.

Junípero Serra had no idea when he was called back to the college that he would remain there for eight years. He longed to do more missionary work, but he never complained or questioned what the church asked of him. He spent much of his time in quiet prayer, but he was in great demand to preach not only in Mexico City but in outlying areas as well.

In the 1700s priests often punished themselves for the sins of the people. Father Serra would sometimes stand in the pulpit of the church and beat his chest with heavy stones. He even whipped himself with chains. Many of those watching him sobbed out loud. In a voice like thunder he warned about punishment and hell. "Help those in need!" he roared. "Do penance for your sins!"

Some people liked Father Serra for having the courage to say what he thought, but others didn't like him, for he made them feel guilty. They didn't want to be reminded of their selfish lives. One evening when the priest was celebrating Mass, he suddenly turned pale and couldn't speak. He had to be carried from the altar and placed on a bed. Someone had poisoned his cup of wine! After Father Serra recovered, he forgave the person who tried to kill him.

In 1767 something happened that changed

the course of Father Serra's life. Until then a catholic order called Jesuits had established missions in Baja California or Lower California. But in 1767 King Carlos III of Spain expelled the Jesuits from their missions. He wanted the Franciscan priests to take over and run the Jesuit missions. The head of the college at San Fernando chose Father President Serra to preside over them.

At the age of fifty-four Father Junípero Serra again left Mexico City and made another long, rugged journey—this time to Baja California.

At that time Europeans believed that California was a great wilderness Spanish explorers had already been there and had claimed the land for Spain. In 1542 the navigator Juan Cabrillo had discovered the Bay of San Diego in the south. And in 1602 the explorer Sebastián Vizcaino, in his search for a harbor, had gone north and discovered Monterey Bay. Vizcaino had placed a large cross under an oak tree and had built an altar and claimed the land for the king of

Spain. The land was then left undisturbed with Indians living in the woods, among the huge redwoods, close to the Pacific Ocean.

In 1769 King Carlos III learned that other countries were showing an interest in California. Russian fur traders were pushing south, looking for furs. And Russian ships had been spotted off the California coast. So were Dutch and English pirate ships! And England was beginning to move westward from her colonies on the eastern coast.

King Carlos III had appointed José de Gálvez to be his representative in Mexico. It was Gálvez who convinced the king that the time had come to send an expedition of soldiers and missionaries to settle upper California—from San Diego to Monterey. Only if the land was occupied by colonists could it legally belong to Spain.

To lead the expedition, Gálvez chose Captain Gaspar de Portolá who was governor of Baja California. Father Serra was chosen to accompany Portolá. Serra and the missionaries would set up missions and convert the Indians. They would also serve the religious needs of all the people at the missions. Portolá and his soldiers would be responsible for protecting the missions from attack by unfriendly Indians. And Spain would gain new land.

Both Portolá and Serra—each with specific goals—were happy to set off on their new adventure!

Trip Through
the Desert

BEFORE BEGINNING THEIR TRIP OF OVER one thousand miles the hundreds of expeditioners had to gather animals—cows, sheep, horses, and mules—and they had to pack food and equipment.

Father Serra had been given permission to gather some sacred articles from the missions in Baja California so that he would be able to set up his new missions and conduct church services. One hundred sixty-three mules carried these religious items and other supplies. There were silver cups and bowls, candlesticks, a large silver cross, pictures of the saints and the Holy Mother, and bells. Father Serra was very fond of bells.

The expeditioners also packed pots, pans, needles, thread, hammers, nails, cups, linens, and many other things. And they packed food that would not spoil. There were figs, dates, salted meats, red chili peppers, chocolate, gallons of wine and water, and one hundred twenty-five pounds of garlic! Father Serra took along plenty of seeds so he could begin sowing crops once they arrived.

In case they met dangerous Indians along the way, the soldiers wore jackets called *cueros* made of a half dozen layers of deerskin, too thick for arrows to pierce. And they carried swords and muskets.

There were other dangers to worry about: steep mountains, deep jungles, dangerous animals, hot deserts. To make certain that at least some of the Spaniards would arrive safely, the expedition split into four groups. Two groups would go by land and two would go by sea. The four groups planned to join up in San Diego.

One ship, the *San Carlos,* left first, followed

by the *San Antonio* a month later. The first land expedition left Baja California a month after that. Father Juan Crespi, a faithful friend of Serra's who came with him from Spain, and a soldier named Francisco Rivera headed the first land group. Captain Portolá and Father Serra's expedition, the last to leave, followed Rivera and Crespi's trail through the wilderness.

Serra had worked so hard preparing for the journey that he was tired when he set out. His sore leg was troubling him again, the same leg that had been bitten years before. It was swollen with a red open sore from the ankle halfway up to the knee. But he would not let the infection stop him from moving on to California.

The expedition was on the road less than a day when the pain became too great for Father Serra to bear. Portolá urged him to return to Mexico City, but the priest wouldn't hear of it. Instead, he devised a cure for himself. He saw a muleteer spreading a yellow ointment over the sores on a mule's back. If the medicine was good for the mule, why not for himself? the priest wondered. He asked the muleteer to provide him with the same ointment for his leg. The man laughed, but agreed to do it. He picked herbs from the ground, crushed them, and mixed them with tallow. Then he applied the mixture to Father Serra's sore leg.

The next morning the priest woke up smiling. His pain was gone. He couldn't walk, but he could ride. Two soldiers lifted him onto an old worn-out mule, and he was on his way again.

The caravan traveled many miles without a sign of an Indian. Then one day about a dozen Indian men appeared at the edge of the woods. Father Serra couldn't believe his eyes. They were as "naked as Adam," he wrote in his diary. He worried about coming across naked Indian women. But his worries were needless, for he reported that the expedition soon met two Indian women who were dressed so decently that he wished all Christian women were as modest.

The caravan met another group of Indians who were very interested in the clothes the white men wore. The Indians tugged on Father Serra's sleeve and begged to have his shabby robe. They even tried to take the breeches off the soldiers!

One Indian was especially curious about Father Serra's eyeglasses. The Indian had never seen glasses before, so the priest took them off and explained what they were. Other Indians came to take a look, and before Father Serra knew it, his eyeglasses had disappeared.

Father Serra was frantic. He depended a great deal on his glasses, and there was no way he could have another pair made in the wilderness. He tramped through the woods, searching, until he came across two young Indian girls sitting under a tree. They were taking turns putting the glasses on their hair, their forehead, and their noses. They thought the glasses were ornaments. When Father Serra asked for his glasses, the Indian girls didn't want to give them up, but they finally did after the friar gave them each a string of beads.

Most of the Indians Father Serra and his

group met were friendly, but once they came across an angry group of Indians. The Indians shouted and waved their arms at the Spaniards, motioning them to retreat. They wanted no trespassers on their land. But when the soldiers fired loud blasts from their muskets, the frightened Indians fled back into the woods.

Father Serra and his companions tramped through tangled woods and over narrow trails. They trudged over barren deserts where the sun sizzled, and hot wind blew sand in their faces. Sometimes they climbed up and down steep hills before reaching level ground on which to pitch camp. After one such long stretch they found a green pasture near a running stream. Here, under brilliant stars, they lay down to rest. But for four nights a mountain lion roared and kept them awake.

Like his companions, Father Serra slept on the ground. His large cross was always on his chest and his prayer book at his side. Every morning when the sun came up, soldiers and workers stood in the wilderness with bowed heads as the little priest recited Mass.

The expeditioners pushed northward until they arrived at the top of a high cliff. The downward path was "so steep that just to look down at it made you shiver," Father Serra wrote in his diary. He wrote that it was one of the few times in his life when he was so frightened he was afraid his heart would stop. It was impossible to ride the mules down the steep path, and it was also very difficult to walk. So the expeditioners and the mules skidded, tumbled, and slid until they all reached the bottom of the steep incline.

At times the expeditioners were short of temper. One day, on a narrow trail, a donkey got in the way of one of the cooks. The two stopped and stared at each other, neither budging an inch. Then, slowly, without taking his eyes from the donkey, the man pulled out a shiny knife from his belt and stabbed the animal. For punishment the cook was ordered to walk the rest of the way.

The caravan had been on the road for

more than three months. The men were discouraged, for the trip seemed endless. They knew that San Diego was close to the Pacific, but they had seen no sign of the ocean. All they had found were walls of mountains and deep ravines.

Then, at the beginning of July 1769, the weary expeditioners caught a glimpse of an ocean in the distance. And as they drew closer, they could see the sails of two ships anchored near the shore and Spanish flags flying in the breeze—the *San Carlos* and the *San Antonio*!

The men shouted with joy, and Father Serra fell to his knees and thanked God for their good fortune.

San Diego

FATHER CRESPI AND RIVERA'S GROUP HAD already arrived in San Diego. Even as the men joyously greeted one another, it became clear to Father Serra and the others that something was terribly wrong. Everyone who had traveled by land arrived in good health. Those who had traveled by sea had not been so lucky, especially the men from the *San Carlos*. Strong winds had blown the ship off course. The water supply had been used up. And when the men stopped to get water at an island, the water was polluted.

Worst of all, most of the men at sea had

developed scurvy. Their gums bled, their teeth fell out, and the men were extremely weak. Although the sailors didn't know it at the time, they got this disease because they hadn't eaten enough vitamin C. They had no fresh vegetables or fruits, especially oranges and lemons. Many of the men died at sea. Many others were so ill they had to be carried off the ships.

A Frenchman named Dr. Prat was in charge of putting together a makeshift hospital which consisted of two tents made from the sails of the ships.

Father Serra and all the others who were well immediately unloaded their mules, unpacked their provisions, and went to help nurse the sick.

A supply ship with food and medicine was on its way from Mexico, but more men died before it arrived. Of the two hundred nineteen people who had left Mexico, only one hundred twenty-six were still alive. At a solemn service Father Serra prayed for the living and said Mass for the dead.

Meanwhile the colonists had to follow

Gálvez's orders and make plans to find Monterey. It was decided that Father Serra would remain in San Diego to build his first mission, and Captain Portolá would lead a land expedition to search for Monterey. Father Crespi and sixty-three other men made up this group. In mid-July they left with enough food and tools to start a new mission in Monterey.

The *San Antonio,* with barely enough sailors to hoist the sails, returned to Mexico. The ship carried letters from Father Serra, pleading for more men and supplies.

Father Serra began the work he'd always dreamed of doing: building his first mission. First he hung a bell from the branch of a tree. Near the bell he placed a cross in the ground. Then, with the help of his men, he built a small church with young trees and branches. He also built simple huts to live in, a place to store supplies, and a barracks for the soldiers who had stayed to protect the mission. With the seeds he had carried from Baja California, Father Serra planted a garden of beans, wheat, and corn.

Eventually some Indians came out of the woods to watch. They were curious about what the priest was doing. Father Serra wanted to talk with them and explain to them about the Catholic religion. He was eager to teach the Indians the prayers of his church. And he wanted to teach them the customs of his own people. But he couldn't speak the Indian language. At first he tried to communicate by giving the Indians gifts he'd brought from Mexico. He gave them shiny glass beads, strips of bright ribbons, pieces of woolen cloth. The Indians loved the presents and wanted to give the priest something. One night they crept into the mission and hung strips of dried fish on the cross.

The Indians had their own religion. They worshiped nature—the sun and the stars, the trees and the wind. They believed that animals had magical powers, so they carved totem poles with pictures of animals to help protect them from evil spirits. The Indians also had their own music and dances. They chanted and performed sun dances, because the sun made all things grow.

Father Serra invited the Indians to visit the little church. He showed them pictures of the Virgin Mary and the Holy Child, and he sang hymns for them. But the priest knew that it would take awhile before he converted the Indians to Christianity.

The Indians, who had always lived off the land, often had just enough food for themselves. When the Spaniards first arrived, however, they, too, had to rely on the land for some of their food. It took the Spaniards a while before they could harvest crops and share them with the Indians. Some of the Indians felt threatened by the newcomers and did what they could to get back at the intruders.

One night when no one was guarding the *San Carlos,* a group of Indians paddled their canoes out to the ship, climbed quietly onboard, and cut pieces out of the sail.

Early one morning during Mass, when few soldiers were on duty, some Indians crept into the mission. Going from hut to hut, they stole clothes, pots, pans, blankets, sheets—anything they could carry. The soldiers, along with the mission blacksmith and carpenter, tried to stop the Indians. The Indians attacked them with clubs and arrows, killing some soldiers. But when the soldiers fired their muskets, the Indians, terrified by the booming sounds, turned and fled. The blacksmith shouted, "Long live the faith! Long live the faith!" as the Indians carried their dead and wounded into the woods.

A few days later the Indians returned as if nothing had happened. They wanted help for their wounded. The soldiers were distrustful, but Father Serra persuaded them to forgive the Indians.

Father Serra continued his efforts to convert the Indians. An Indian boy who was staying at the mission had learned some Spanish. With sign language and the boy's help, Father Serra began teaching catechism and the Lord's Prayer to the Indians. But few of them came to learn. Junípero Serra thought he was making some progress when an Indian father asked him to baptize his infant son. A crowd of Indians watched as the gentle priest took the child in his arms and prayed. But just as Father Serra was about to pour the holy water over the child, the Indian father became frightened. He snatched his baby from the priest and ran away, with the onlookers following him.

Serra faced other problems as well. A new attack of scurvy was plaguing the mission, and he, too, was suffering from it. The supply ship with food and medicine from Mexico City had not yet arrived. And there was no news about Captain Portolá and his expedition to Monterey.

The Search for Monterey

SIX MONTHS WENT BY BEFORE CAPTAIN Portolá and his men returned to the mission in San Diego. The men were exhausted and starving. They had once been so desperate for food that they had killed some of their mules and eaten them. Many of the men had developed scurvy.

In addition, Portolá had failed to find Monterey—at least, he thought he had failed. He had followed the map of explorer Vizcaino, which led him to the beautiful bay. Portolá just didn't recognize it from Vizcaino's map. So Portolá and his men just kept going north. On the way, they discovered spectacular San Francisco Bay, but this discovery had no meaning for them at the time.

After the men had had time to rest, Father Serra told Portolá that since Gálvez had ordered them to start missions in both San Diego and Monterey, they must begin another search for Monterey.

Portolá, who had had enough exploring, refused. He argued, saying that there wasn't enough food for another expedition. He also suspected that since the *San Antonio* had not returned in over a year, it was probably lost. Portolá did not want to go on a fool's search. If he was going anywhere, it was home to Mexico!

Father Serra was disappointed. He had not made a single convert in San Diego. And if Portolá did not find Monterey, he feared that Spain would lose California and the Indians would lose God.

Father Serra wouldn't accept defeat. He begged Portolá to wait and pray. The feast of Saint Joseph, a patron saint, was nine days away, and Father Serra suggested that the men pray every day until then. For eight days they prayed and watched the sea. On the ninth day, the day of the feast of Saint Joseph, they saw the sail of a ship! But when the sun set, the ship disappeared in the darkness.

Everyone felt their prayers had gone unanswered—but not Father Serra. He continued to pray.

Five days later the *San Antonio* pulled into the harbor! Now there were food and supplies, and now the men could once again set out on their search for Monterey.

This time, Father Serra went with the expedition. He traveled by sea. On April 17, 1770, he wrote his friend Father Palou in Mexico City: "The captain sent word to embark, and I gladly obeyed." In the letter Father Serra asked Father Palou to send candles and incense for the new church he would build in Monterey.

Portolá went by land to look for Monterey. The captain and his men found the journey to be much easier this time. Food

was not a problem, and since it was spring-time, they could follow landmarks more easily. They joyously discovered the oak tree where the explorer Vizcaino had built an altar almost one hundred and seventy years before! Remnants of the altar were still standing. Nearby the explorers located the beautiful oval-shaped harbor of Monterey.

Portolá's men lit watchfires to guide Father Serra's ship. Eight days later the priest came ashore and found an altar and a bell already hanging from the branch of a tree!

In the wilderness, between ocean and forest, Father Serra conducted a beautiful religious ceremony. Two processions marched toward the little church in the woods: one from the sea, the other from the land. The priest, dressed in a purple robe with gold threads that glittered in the sun, sang High Mass. The pioneers knelt before the cross and thanked God for their good fortune. The flag of Spain was unfurled while everyone cheered and shouted at the top of their voices: "Long live the king! Long live the king!"

Portolá took a handful of earth from the ground and threw it as far as he could. He claimed the land for Spain.

When the ceremonies were over, everyone went to the beach and enjoyed a huge banquet. Then Father Serra and his men returned to the ship, and the others returned to their camp along the Carmel River. At last Monterey officially belonged to Spain.

A few days later Captain Portolá sailed for Mexico City. When he arrived, there was a great celebration. The streets were lined with crowds of people waiting to greet the explorer.

Father Serra stayed in Monterey with others because he was eager to begin building a new mission.

Monterey

SERRA MISSED THE GOOD-NATURED POR-
tolá. Captain Pedro Fages was now the
officer in command at Monterey. This mean,
bad-tempered young man couldn't get along
with Serra or the Indians or even his soldiers.
He opened Serra's mail and read it. He beat
the Indians for the slightest mistakes they
made. He treated the soldiers so cruelly that
they hated him.

Father Serra knew that his present mission
would fail if he didn't protect the Indians
and separate them from Fages and his soldiers. So he decided to separate the mission

from the barracks by finding a new place for the mission.

Father Serra and his friend Father Juan Crespi explored the area until they found a spot about five miles away on the little Bay of Carmel. Tall pine and oak trees shaded the fertile green land, and the Carmel River flowed close by. Food could easily grow here. It was just the right place to start a new mission.

Father Serra named the new mission, Mission San Carlos de Monterey, and carpenters began to build a church. They also built huts for Father Serra and Father Crespi and any visitors that might come from Mexico. Father Serra decorated the little church with the sacred objects he had carried over the long journey. On the whitewashed walls he hung pictures of the saints and the Holy Mother. He adorned the altar with a large cross and two fine silver candlesticks. Later the Indians brought flowers and painted colorful pictures on the walls to make the church more beautiful.

Father Serra's little room was furnished with a bed made of boards, a blanket, a stool, and a table with a candle and a quill. That was all he wanted for himself: a place to sleep and a table on which to write.

The Indians at Carmel were a friendly tribe. When Father Serra rang the bell for early morning Mass, many came. The priest blessed each one and made the sign of the cross. Then he gave them each a bowl of hot cereal made of wheat or Indian cornmeal.

Little by little, Father Serra learned the language of the tribe. Every day he learned new words and phrases, and each night in his little room he repeated them until he could say them almost as well as the Indians did. It was hard work.

Teaching Spanish to the Indians was also difficult. Father Serra would gather them together under a tree and start each lesson with the words *Amor a Dios,* which means "Love God." Soon Indians and Spaniards were greeting each other on the roads with *"Amor a Dios."* The Indians learned a few words and phrases at a time. When they could finally recite prayers and sing hymns in Spanish, Father Serra was grateful.

Like the Pame Indians in Serra Gorda, the Carmel Indians loved the Catholic ceremonies and processions with candlelight and banners. They also grew to love Father Serra—the young Indians called him "the old father."

Father Serra tried to teach the Indians to hoe and plant, but they preferred the life of the forest. When they needed food, the Indians hunted deer and rabbit, or they picked berries from bushes and acorns from the ground. The men made sharp cutting tools of shell and hard stone. The women wove fine baskets out of tall grass and used them for cooking and serving their families. When their homes of branches and twigs became dirty, the Indians burned them down and built new ones. The Indians sang and danced to the music of homemade flutes and drums. To them, life in the forest seemed preferable to life at the mission.

Father Serra worried about the Indians

going naked. He wanted the children to learn to wear clothes, so he had brightly colored cloth sent from Mexico. He became an expert tailor and taught the Indian women to sew and make pretty dresses for the girls and shirts and pants for the boys. The children seemed to take great delight in their new clothes.

Father Serra especially wanted the children to come to the mission. One day, when a ship stopped in the harbor, a friendly sailor gave the priest a mother hen and her chicks. Serra showed the chickens to the Indian children, who had never seen such animals before. Every day the children came to feed the chickens and watch them grow. Then one day an Indian woman and her son stole the new pets and ate them.

There was not enough food to feed the colonists and the "neophytes" who had moved to the mission. The supply ship had not come for a year. And since the garden had just been planted, it would be awhile until harvest time.

Father Serra prayed for a solution to the

food shortage—and his prayers were answered when Fages suggested a bear hunt! Fages said that there were many bears in a deep ravine not too far away. He had once been to the ravine and had named it the Valley of the Bears. These bears would make fine food, Fages said.

Fages took off with the thirteen soldiers who were his best shots, and for six months they killed bears and sent the meat back to the mission.

Finally, after more than a year, the supply ship arrived. It brought food and supplies—and ten more missionaries! Father Serra could now move on!

San Gabriel

WITH TEN MORE MISSIONARIES FATHER Serra decided to start five new missions. He wanted to send two friars to each new mission because one man by himself would get too lonely. A whole year would pass before a visitor or a letter would arrive!

First, Father Serra asked Fages and two of the new friars to start Mission San Gabriel. Then Father Serra and two other friars set up Mission San Antonio. They built the new mission in a beautiful valley surrounded by rugged mountains and filled with tall oaks. Grapes and nuts grew all around. It was only a day's walk from Mission San Carlos. Father Serra wanted the missions to be a day's distance from each other in case there was ever any trouble. He also wanted them close so that weary travelers would have places to stop each night during their journeys. He had remembered how difficult it was walking those many miles between missions in Baja California.

Before the church in San Antonio was built, Father Serra hung a bell from the branch of a great oak. He rang the bell and shouted, "Come to the Holy church! Come! Come to receive the faith of Jesus Christ."

The two other missionaries asked Father Serra why he was ringing the bell. There wasn't an Indian in sight. "They will come!" Serra said. "They will come!" And they did: First one Indian crept out of the woods, and then another.

Father Serra was pleased with this mission. The Indians were friendly, and the soil was rich and would yield good crops. By this time four missions had been been started: Mission San Diego was started in

1769; San Carlos Mission in Carmel near Monterey in 1770; San Antonio de Padua in 1771; and San Gabriel also in 1771.

Suddenly bad news came to Father Serra from Mission San Gabriel, where Captain Fages was in charge. The Indians of San Gabriel had been peaceful and friendly. They had even thought the Spaniards were gods, for they had seen them strike stones together and make fire! But then disaster struck. A soldier shot and wounded the wife of an Indian chief. The chief was furious and wanted revenge. He and his braves attacked the soldiers. The soldiers fought back, killing a number of Indians, including the chief. The soldiers then cut off the head of the dead chief and stuck it on a pole over the gate.

Fages failed to punish the soldier who had caused the trouble or to discipline the others. When Father Serra heard what had happened in San Gabriel, he rushed there and tried to make Fages understand the importance of keeping peace with the Indians. But Fages wouldn't listen to him. He wouldn't allow anyone to interfere with his command.

Father Serra left San Gabriel greatly disturbed.

When he arrived in Carmel, he sat in his hut and thought about all of his problems: There was never enough food. There was trouble with the Indians, and Fages was violent and unpredictable. Many of his soldiers deserted and fled into the forest. If the soldiers continued to leave, the missions would surely fail.

Father Serra would not be defeated. He had heard that Viceroy Bucareli, the highest officer in Mexico, was a good man who cared a great deal about colonizing California. Serra decided to return to Mexico and ask Bucareli to help him.

Father Serra was sixty years old. His sore leg pained him constantly, and he suffered from asthma, which made breathing hard for him. Neverthless, he decided to make the rugged two-thousand-mile trip to Mexico City.

With an eleven-year-old Indian boy as his helper, Father Serra set out. They went by sea and land. On their way to Mexico City they both became ill with very high fevers. Serra prayed for the boy. He was especially concerned because he knew that if the boy died, the Indians back home might think that the Spaniards had killed him. The boy did pull through, and the two weak and thin travelers arrived safely in Mexico City.

Father Serra and the boy went to Viceroy Bucareli's palace. The boy had never seen such luxury before: heavy draperies embroidered with gold thread, carved chairs, shining tables, and huge beautiful pictures in gilded frames.

A servant led Father Serra to Bucareli's chamber. Though the little priest wore an old gray robe and sandals, the viceroy welcomed him with great respect. He knew that Father Serra cared about the missions as much as he did. He listened carefully to the pale old friar who spoke passionately about his work in California.

Father Serra spoke with a strong and forceful voice as he presented his requests to Bucareli. He wanted families to settle in California. He wanted blacksmiths, carpenters, and people who knew about agriculture to come to the missions to teach their skills to the Indians. He asked for a doctor because Dr. Prat, who had been the missions' doctor, had died. And he requested a raise in salary for the hard-working friars. With money the friars could order things from Mexico City—sandals, pens, paper, and other things to make their lives more comfortable. Father Serra always gave away his own salary as soon as he received it.

Finally Father Serra asked that all captains be given orders not to interfere with the work of the missionaries. And he asked that Captain Fages be removed from his job. The viceroy promised to consider Father Serra's requests and to give him all the help he could.

The priest was satisfied as he sailed back to Carmel. With the generous help of Viceroy Bucareli, he thought that the missions would survive. Bucareli used his own personal funds to pay for shiploads of food and supplies for the missions. Father Serra was also delighted because his longtime friend,

Father Palou, was leaving Mexico to come and work with him.

Father Serra returned to Mission San Carlos in Carmel just in time. The settlers were close to starvation. They had been living on milk and herbs, without even bread to eat. Thanks to Bucareli's kindness, Father Serra had brought back food and supplies, including five bales of cotton to make the Indian children new clothes!

San Francisco

IN 1772 FATHER SERRA FOUNDED HIS FIFTH mission in San Luis Obispo. The sixth one was to be nearby in San Francisco, an excellent location, because mission soldiers could guard the coastline against enemies from the north. And ships could easily maneuver in and out of the large, safe harbor.

Francisco Rivera was now the military commander of the missions. He started the search for a mission site.

Father Serra had asked Viceroy Bucareli to send families to California, and now they were coming. Two hundred and forty people—farmers and tradesmen and their families—were on their way from Mexico, traveling over narrow trails and high hills, through floods and storms. A baby was born on top of a snow-covered mountain, and more babies were born farther along the way. It was freezing cold, but that did not stop the pioneers. All of them, including the newborn children, survived.

The settlers came with clothes, blankets, shoes for the children, and ribbons for the women. They carried six yards of ribbon for every woman! These ladies would be the best-dressed women in the wilderness.

The Indians seemed glad to see their new neighbors. They exchanged gifts: The Spaniards gave beads to the Indians, and the Indians gave clams and seeds to the Spaniards.

From the hills of San Francisco the pioneers could look down upon a shining bay that was as quiet as a lake. It was on this site near the sea and mountains that the new mission and presidio (fort) were built. And Father Serra chose his friends Father Palou and Father Crespi to run the mission. On

September 17, 1776, three months after the Declaration of Independence was signed in Philadelphia, Father Francisco Palou with Father Juan Crespi sang the first Mass in San Francisco.

Meanwhile, south of San Francisco, near Mission San Diego, Father Serra was building his seventh mission, the beautiful Mission San Juan Capistrano. This mission was surrounded by tangled vines of wild grapes and large fields of roses. Father Serra thought it was the loveliest place he had ever seen. A year later, in 1777, the friar established Mission Santa Clara near San Francisco. And a few years after that he started Mission San Buenaventura, his last.

During the fifteen years that he was in California, Father Serra built nine missions. He named all of them after Catholic saints. From north to south, along the Pacific coast, the missions were: San Francisco, Santa Clara, San Carlos, San Antonio de Padua, San Luis Obispo, San Buenaventura, San Gabriel, San Juan Capistrano, and San Diego.

Father Serra kept busy maintaining and improving conditions at the missions. At one mission some teenage Indian boys were causing trouble. They disliked farming and were disruptive. Father Serra knew that the boys liked to work with animals, so he asked someone to teach them how to become *vaqueros,* or cowboys. The boys learned to brand cows and ride horses and throw lassos. They went into the forest and lassoed the wild pumas, bears, and coyotes that pounced on men and cattle. The boys were doing what they liked and were no longer getting into mischief.

Then a more serious problem began to emerge. Father Serra's work with the Indians was threatened by his own countrymen.

Spain was at war with England, and only a few colonists were coming to California to build towns and carry on trade. And missionaries were no longer coming to convert Indians. Governor Neve now ruled over California. Viceroy Bucareli had died, and when Father Serra wrote to the new viceroy in Mexico City, asking for protection for his mission, his letter was never answered. Soon trouble began.

The Yuma Indians had lived peacefully along the coast of California for generations and had planted fields of corn and beans and melons. They rode fine horses; it was said that the women rode as well as the men. But when the Spanish colonists arrived, they trampled over the Yuma's fields and destroyed their crops. The missionaries had always brought gifts to the Indians, but these Spaniards brought nothing. Instead, they took the most fertile land for themselves. And when the Yumas protested, the Spaniards refused to listen.

One Sunday the Yumas attacked the Spaniards. They burned every home and killed every man. They did not hurt the women and children, but took them back to their village to work in their homes and fields.

After the Yuma Massacre the missionaries were blamed—at least, in part—for causing the Indian hostility. The government thought that the missionaries were gaining too much power. To avoid another uprising Governor Neve used his authority to prevent Father Serra from building a mission in Santa Barbara. Instead Neve built only a military presidio there. (Four years later, however, after Father Serra died, the Santa Barbara mission was built.)

Neve and Father Serra often argued. Neve had ideas about what the missionaries should and should not do. Father Serra had his own ideas!

The End of the Road

IN 1784, WHEN HE WAS SEVENTY-ONE YEARS old, Father Serra started on a trip, visiting the nine missions he had built. He was weak and in bad health, but he felt that he still had much work to do, for many Indians had not yet been converted.

The bells rang out whenever Father Serra arrived at a mission. Everyone crowded around him, happy to see their faithful friend.

All nine of the missions seemed to be doing well. Indians were working in the fields. Many of them had become skilled

farmers and workmen and were being paid for their work. Father Serra was glad to hear that the Indians were receiving the same pay as the other workers. New schools had been built and were filled with Indian children learning the Spanish language as well as Catholic hymns and prayers.

The missionaries were often lonely and discouraged, but Father Serra tried to cheer them up and give them the courage to go on.

At every mission the Indians came to Father Serra and asked to be baptized. There were now about seven thousand Indians in California who had become Christians.

After traveling five hundred miles from mission to mission, Father Serra returned to Carmel. He was exhausted, and his bad leg was giving him a great deal of trouble. "I have come home to die," he told his friends.

Before he died, he wanted to do one more thing for the Indian children. A ship had recently brought colorful cloth to the mission, so Father Serra cut it up to make clothes for the boys and girls. Then he sent a letter to his dearest friend, Father Palou, in San

Francisco and asked him to come. Father Palou left San Francisco immediately.

When he arrived in Carmel, he found Father Serra in church, singing. Palou said to the soldier on duty, "It doesn't seem that the Father is very sick."

The soldier answered, "There is no hope. He is ill. This saintly priest is always well when he is praying or singing, but he is dying."

Father Palou brought Father Serra back to his hut and placed him on his bed. Then, on August 28, 1784, Father Serra died, holding the large cross he had brought from Spain thirty-four years before.

The mission bells tolled the sad news. Soldiers, sailors, Indians, and colonists left their work and came together to mourn. Mass was sung in the little church crowded with people. Indians covered the coffin with roses, and as the coffin was laid into the earth, sounds of sobbing filled the air.

Epilogue

TODAY FATHER SERRA IS CONSIDERED TO have been a kind and faithful friend of the Indians. If you visit California, you will see statues of him in Monterey, Malibu, and in Golden Gate Park in San Francisco. Another statue stands in the Capitol in Washington, D.C. In 1963, to commemorate his 250th birthday, Father Serra was honored with a national medal—the first Catholic priest to be so honored.

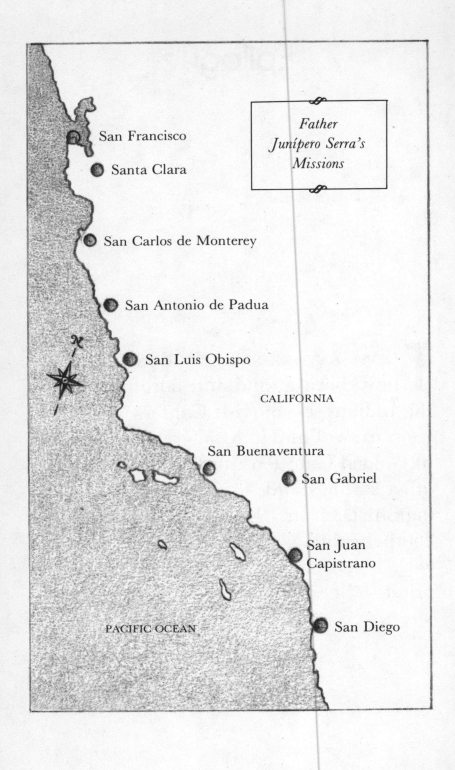

Father
*Junípero Serra's
Missions*

San Francisco

Santa Clara

San Carlos de Monterey

San Antonio de Padua

San Luis Obispo

CALIFORNIA

San Buenaventura

San Gabriel

San Juan
Capistrano

PACIFIC OCEAN

San Diego

FATHER JUNÍPERO SERRA'S MISSIONS

Mission San Diego,
founded July 16, 1769

Mission San Carlos de Monterey,
founded June 3, 1770

Mission San Antonio de Padua,
founded July 14, 1771

Mission San Gabriel,
founded September 8, 1771

Mission San Luis Obispo,
founded September 1, 1772

Mission San Francisco,
founded October 9, 1776

Mission San Juan Capistrano,
founded November 1, 1776

Mission Santa Clara,
founded January 18, 1777

Mission San Buenaventura,
founded March 31, 1782

Highlights in the Life of
FATHER JUNÍPERO SERRA

1713   On November 24, Miguel José Serra is born to Antonio and Margarita Serra. He is baptized immediately because he was born small and weak.

He learns prayers and hymns at an early age from going to church every evening with his mother. When he is a little older, he attends a religious school, where Franciscan priests teach him religion, history, geography, and Latin.

He grows up and attends college at Lullian University.

1731   On September 15, Miguel José Serra becomes a Franciscan friar and changes his name to *Junípero*, a companion of Saint Francis.

1749   Father Serra arrives in Vera Cruz, Mexico, on December 6.

1750   On January 1, after a lengthy, perilous journey on foot, Father Serra reaches the gates of the College of San Fernando in Mexico City. Soon, he begins his training for missionary work there.

In May, Father Serra leaves for Sierra Gorda to work with the Pame Indians. He is named Father President of the region.

95

1758 Father Serra returns to the College of San Fernando.

1767 Father Serra leaves for Baja California to preside over the missions vacated by the Jesuits.

1769 Father Serra begins his journey to California and establishes his first mission in San Diego on July 16.

1784 Father Serra dies on August 28 at the San Carlos de Monterey Mission, where he is buried.

For Further Study

More Books to Read

Father Junípero Serra, the Traveling Missionary. Linda Lyngheim (Langtrey Press)

Junípero Serra. Sean Dolan (Chelsea House)

Junípero Serra. Marion A. Habig (Franciscan Press)

Never Turn Back: Father Serra's Mission. James J. Rawls (Raintree Steck-Vaughn)

Sally and Father Serra. Sarah Duque (Tabor Publishing)

Serra's San Diego: Father Junípero Serra and California's Beginnings. Iris H. Engstrand (San Diego Historical Society)

Videos

The Missions. (Agency for Instructional Technology)

The Missions. (Video Knowledge, Inc.)

The Missions: Mission Life and Missions of the Southwest. (Bennu Productions, Inc)

Index

EAST ORANGE PUBLIC LIBRARY
The story of Junipero Serra : brave ad
Jr.Dept. B Serra / White, Florence M

3 2665 0014 6445 4

DISCARD